THE
BROKEN
BADGE

THE BROKEN BADGE

RETHINKING POLICE & COMMUNITY RELATIONS IN AMERICA

COL. KL WILLIAMS, *CHIEF OF POLICE*

For information about this title or to order other books and/or electronic media, contact the publisher:

KL Williams
336 36th Street, Suite 725
Bellingham Washington 98225
www.instituteofja.com
klwms007@gmail.com

ISBNs:
Print: 978-0-9998075-0-7
eBook: 978-0-9998075-1-4

Printed in the United States of America

Not everything that is faced can be changed, but nothing can be changed until it is faced.

—*JAMES BALDWIN*

TABLE OF CONTENTS

THE BROKEN BADGE

INTRODUCTION

During the summer of 1990 I had the opportunity to ride along with the Los Angeles police department. The officer I rode with worked extensively in the community and shared this story with me. He stated that when he started his patrol that day he noticed a young African American male about four years old playing in front of his house. He stopped to talk to the young boy. Suddenly the child's mother ran out, grabbed the child, and told him that's the enemy—never speak to them.

This is where we begin.

LAW ENFORCEMENT OATH OF HONOR

On my honor, I would never betray my badge,
my integrity, my character, or the public trust.

I will always have the courage to hold myself
and others accountable for our actions.

I will always uphold the Constitution, my community,
and the agency I serve.
—FROM THE INTERNATIONAL ASSOCIATION
OF CHIEFS OF POLICE

Police officers do a very difficult job under difficult circumstances and most often do the job well. I have been honored to have been a police officer for the greater part of my career. I believe it is a career that is full of dignity, respect, and a true commitment to public service. I have often said that a police officer's duty involves a willingness to risk their life to save people they don't even know. If that is not an honorable profession I do not know what is.

If all police officers followed the aforementioned law enforcement oath of honor day in and day out I wonder if we would have as many difficulties in American policing as we do today.

When the color of a person's skin is seen as a weapon they are always considered armed and dangerous.

—*Unknown*

CHAPTER 1

RULES OF ENGAGEMENT

Rules or directives to military forces including individuals that define the circumstances, conditions, degree, and manner in which the use of force or actions, which might be construed as provocative, may be applied. They provide authorization for and/or limits on, among other things, the use of force and the employment of certain specific capabilities. In some nations rules of engagement have the status of guidance to military forces while in other nations rules of engagement are lawful commands. Rules of engagement do not normally dictate how a result is to be achieved but will indicate what measures may be acceptable.

While rules of engagement are used in both domestic and international operations by most militaries, rules of engagement are not used for domestic operations in the United States. Instead the use of force by the U.S. military in such situations is governed by the rules of the use of force.

An abbreviated description of the rules of engagement may be issued to all personnel. Commonly referred to as a rule of engagement card, this document provides the soldier with a summary of the rules of engagement regulating the use of force for mission.

ABOVE EXCERPTED FROM THE U.S. ARMY'S ROE HANDBOOK

Why do some communities today in America see police departments as the enemy and often certain police departments see the community as their enemy? Before any meaningful change can occur, we must get clear in our minds that in America we are not at war with our citizens. In many minority communities in America there has been an ongoing belief that the police do not have the citizens' best interests at heart. Various government programs have focused on arresting black citizens who disagree with police and government policies. This has led to a level of distrust that has made it difficult to develop meaningful positive relationships. It is said that perception is reality to the perceiver. If members of minority communities believe that law enforcement is in some way out to get them, they will not be inclined to help law enforcement even though it is often in their best interest to do so. We must change this paradigm and create a relationship between the community and law enforcement that is of mutual benefit.

American police officers are governed by the United States Constitution. In addition, each police department has a variety of special orders, general orders, and directives which govern the actions and behaviors of each officer as they perform their duty. Most departments update these special orders on a regular basis and make sure each officer understands the intent of each order.

THESE ARE THE FIRST TEN AMENDMENTS TO THE UNITED STATES CONSTITUTION

1. Freedom of religion, speech, press, assembly, and petition
2. Right to keep and bear arms in order to maintain a well-regulated militia
3. No quartering of soldiers
4. Freedom from unreasonable searches and seizures
5. Right to due process of law, freedom from self-incrimination, double jeopardy
6. Rights of accused person, (e.g., right to a speedy and public trial)
7. Right of trial by jury in civil cases
8. Freedom from excessive bail, cruel and unusual punishments
9. Other rights of the people
10. Powers reserved to the states

CHAPTER 2

THE AFTER-PARTY

During the last two weeks of high school, my good friend Kyle and I decided to attend an after-party one Saturday night. We were very excited about graduating from high school and moving on to our new lives. For me that meant moving to California and starting college. Kyle's father had let us use his vehicle. To get to the party, we had to go through the city of Jennings, Missouri. There were some communities in the St. Louis, Missouri, area that we always knew had issues with people of color, and driving through them, especially at night, could be very challenging. When we were in Jennings, a police officer's vehicle suddenly pulled in behind us with red lights and siren blaring. Kyle pulled over and waited while the officer approached. The officer claimed to have seen some type of traffic violation and demanded we produce our identification. Kyle gave him his ID and I gave him mine. After a few minutes the police officer came back, opened the door, grabbed Kyle, and took him to the back of the police car, telling him, "Williams, you are under arrest." Kyle said, "I'm not Williams. That's Williams in the vehicle." Before you could snap your fingers, the officers returned to the vehicle, told me to get out, placed me in handcuffs, and put me in the back of their patrol car.

The officers then said I had stolen a car and was wanted for grand theft auto. Not knowing what they were referring to, there was not much I could say. Then suddenly the officers began demeaning me and laughing, saying, "Nigger, we got you now."

On the way to the police station the officers used racial epithets toward me and yelled. We got to the Jennings police station, and both officers brought me into the station to the booking area. One officer started the booking process, which included fingerprints and photographs. After a few minutes two officers escorted me upstairs in handcuffs to the lobby of the police station. This area was isolated, and no one was there. It was about 1 AM. The officers took me to an area about ten feet from the front door and left me in handcuffs. I stood there wondering what was going on, not knowing what was about to happen. All this time I had been a good student in high school; in fact, an A-student. I had participated in sports, I worked a part-time job, had never been arrested, and by all accounts played by the rules.

After about ten minutes of standing there, three officers peeked around the corner at me and then said, "Damn, boy, we wanted you to run so we could smoke you." Smoke means kill you.

Well, my mother did not raise a fool. There was no way I was going to run out of the police station in handcuffs. I asked myself why these officers wanted to smoke me or kill me. I had done nothing wrong. My friend and I were on our way to a party and that was it. Some officers, I think, find it sporting to want to hurt others for no more reason than their own sadistic amusement. Is it racism or some other bizarre inner drive?

The officers escorted me back to the holding area, placed me in a cell with another individual, and chuckled. After a few hours one of the officers came back and asked me if I had a sister named Zelda, to which I replied no. The officers then decided I was not the subject they were looking for and released me. I went home and told my mom about the experience. She said, "Let that be a lesson for you." I believe it was at that moment I realized subconsciously that if I could change police behavior it would have to be from the inside as a police officer.

THE TABLE LEG

After graduating from the police academy, the young officer is quickly indoctrinated into the philosophies of what it takes to be a police officer for the department they work for. My department, the St. Louis City Police Department, had a long history and tradition. When you graduate from the police academy you go through a variety of training modules. You learn about patrol tactics, criminal investigation, the Constitution, traffic enforcement, defensive tactics, and a multitude of other subjects.

In defensive tactics, we were taught that if we must use the impact weapon or nightstick we strike nerve motor points, which are areas of the body that cause motor/muscle dysfunction, thus ending the conflict. Well, when I hit the streets of St. Louis, I was taught a few other things, too.

When you graduate from the police academy you are issued an assortment of items: your uniform, duty belt, firearm, impact weapon, etc. Today, officers are also issued pepper spray and Tasers.

We were taught in the Academy that strikes to the head, throat, and collarbone were considered deadly force. During my first few days on the street, officers would approach me and tell me to get rid of that department-issued nightstick and purchase a table leg. A table leg is a large piece of wood fashioned as a nightstick with a large chunk of metal on the end. This was the preferred impact weapon prior to and during the late 1980s, the time during which I graduated from the police academy. You are also instructed that if you do have to engage a subject who is resisting you, your primary target is the head. In fact, if you did not strike the subject in the head you were looked at as if you were just playing with the subject. The officers would quickly tell you to give that person a turban. A turban meant to strike that subject in the head with enough force so that when medical attention was applied, the head would have to be wrapped in such a fashion that it looked like the person was wearing a turban, almost as if they were some type of Sultan.

As a point of information, it is important to note that at the beginning of each shift, roll call and inspection of all officers were handled prior to the officers responding to their assigned patrol vehicle. Often, I would watch officers once they left the station and headed to their vehicles grabbing other items to use while they were working. I have observed officers responding to calls with ax handles, brass knuckles, lead-lined gloves, as well as claw hammers. It is also important to note that none of these aforementioned items were department issued or approved.

As a student in the police academy I was always fascinated with defensive tactics. At that time, defensive tactics were going through a transition or crossroads because many of the older officers truly felt that if a subject resisted you, they were to be struck in the head until resistance stopped. My training in the police academy in defensive tactics focused on a variety of areas, wrist locks, joint control, countermeasures, empty hand control, the carotid neck restraint, ground fighting, as well as use of the impact weapon, etc. When I graduated from the academy I wanted to follow the training I was taught. In fact, a few years after graduation I was offered an opportunity to become a defensive tactics instructor for the St. Louis Police Department, to which I was very happy to respond.

When you graduate from the academy you are quickly indoctrinated into a philosophy that if you do not toe the line, you are going to face challenges. Most young officers quickly want to become respected veteran officers. Some officers blindly follow the instruction of senior officers without ever questioning the validity, legality, or morality of the things they are asked to do.

Even today when we look at the multitude of situations where individuals appear to be the victims of excessive force by police officers, one can only ask why. Too many times excessive force is witnessed by other officers but goes unchecked. When asked one time what officers can do to change the high level of excessive force between officers and the citizens, I was able to offer a few solutions.

I think back to Homeland Security during the Boston bombing when they recommended to the citizens that if they see something, say something. As a police officer, I share that and suggest that if officers witness something excessive, they should not just say something, but do something. Step in to stop the resistive situation. We all know that all too often if an officer tries to stop another officer from using excessive force, he is quickly challenged.

This officer may face disciplinary action by the department or face sanctions by the other officers or ridicule and be looked at with disdain. Often some officers wind up losing their jobs, get transferred to another division, or face some other type of repercussion.

When an officer believes that doing the right thing will threaten their position in their chosen profession, many times they choose not to act. It is very sad when doing the right thing causes issues to the point that you may lose your job.

We must keep in mind that there are those individuals in the community who believe they can gun down police officers without fear of repercussions. Even as I write this book two police officers were both shot in the face, in different states, within a week of each other while in their vehicles on patrol. This is not the answer to this very challenging problem. If members of the community seek to take the law into their own hands, it will only escalate into a situation where the public will soon see that violence is not the answer. We must learn to work together, find solutions, and rebuild our community, realizing that we are working together, both law enforcement and the community. Police officers and members of the community must both be held accountable for their actions.

SHARK FRENZY

Every police officer, both young and old, must know their strengths as well as their weaknesses. There will be times in a police officer's career where the use of force will be necessary. It is during these times that all police officers must work toward keeping a calm head as well as acting in the most professional manner possible.

I learned a valuable lesson as a young police officer engaging subjects who were involved in criminal activity. I remember like it was yesterday. My partner and I responded to a call for drug sales at an area known for illegal drug activity night and day. As we approached the scene several subjects took off running. We were able to apprehend most of the subjects and placed them in custody. As I approached one of the subjects' vehicle, three other subjects remained inside. I saw one subject in the backseat unconscious. As I looked in the vehicle I could see various items of drug paraphernalia used for smoking crack. As I attempted to get the backseat passenger out of the vehicle he suddenly struck me in the nose with his fist. I was startled at this, as I was using one of my special defensive tactics techniques of vehicle extraction to safely get the subject from the vehicle. Unknown to me at the time the individual who struck me had been recently released from state prison on a murder conviction.

As the blood spewed from my nose I suddenly saw red and unleashed a barrage of kicks to this individual rendering him dazed and under control. My colleagues at the scene told me that I almost kicked this individual over the car. One factor that was quite apparent, though, is that during this encounter with this subject I lost sight of what was going on and could only feel my rage. The officers told me that as they kept trying to calm me down I continued moving into a martial arts stance and was waiting for someone to enter my personal space. Anyone entering this space was going to be dispensed with through the martial arts skills I practiced daily.

Once I regained my composure, I realized that I cannot allow myself to lose sight of my objective, and I must remain calm until the situation is brought under control. It was at that time I realized that I suffered from what I call shark frenzy. From my point of view, shark frenzy is when an individual loses sight or control of a physical situation and begins fighting in a manner that some would say is dangerous and out of control. At that time, I was a defensive tactics instructor for the St. Louis Police Department, and I knew that in order to maintain that position I was going to have to get a handle on what I believed to be shark frenzy. Through training and meditation, I was able to get a handle on it, and to this day I have never had another incident like the one I just described.

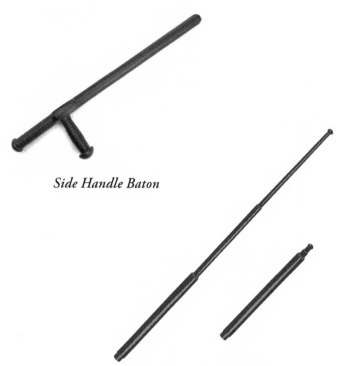

Side Handle Baton

Expandable Baton

Straight-Handle Baton

CHAPTER 3

THE 15 15 70 RULE

IN 1995 I attended a conference hosted by the International Association of Chiefs of Police on the topic of ethics in law enforcement. This conference brought police officers from around the country together to Washington, DC, to look at ethics in law enforcement and how it impacts the community. During this training one area was especially important to me and it was identified as the 15 15 70 rule.

The 15 15 70 rule explains how officers in major police departments function during the course of their duty. This rule basically says that in every major police department 15 percent of the officers are going to be honest and fair. Another 15 percent are going to be dishonest, which could include planting drugs and weapons, manipulating evidence, using excessive force, violating civil rights of individuals, as well as various other corrupt activity. Finally, 70 percent of the officers could go either way depending on who trained them or who's watching them.

For me it is shocking to think that 70 percent of the officers of a major police department could function within the scope of the law honestly or could operate from a corrupt and dishonest standpoint depending on who's watching them or who trained them. I was never fully clear on what defined a major police department. Was it a department of one thousand officers or a department of one hundred officers? I would hope that since this conference occurred decades ago, conditions would have changed. However, in reflecting upon current events around the country, it appears to me that much of this statistical information still rings true.

As an example, if you had a thousand-officer police department and 15 percent of these officers operated from a dishonest or corrupt standpoint, that would mean you have one hundred fifty officers working around the clock who are constantly and systematically destroying the public trust. If these officers are indeed corrupt—manipulating evidence, using excessive force, and violating individual's constitutional rights—how long do you think it would take before the community's trust and confidence in their local police department erode?

If American policing is to truly change, we absolutely must rid departments of what is sometimes termed bad apples. The concept of one bad apple spoiling the bunch certainly rings true in American law enforcement. It doesn't matter if the officer has a racist agenda, corrupt agenda, or personal agenda; we must hold police officers accountable, and they must function squarely within the letter of the law.

This is a segment of the 2010 National Police Misconduct Statistics and Reporting Project (NPMSRP).

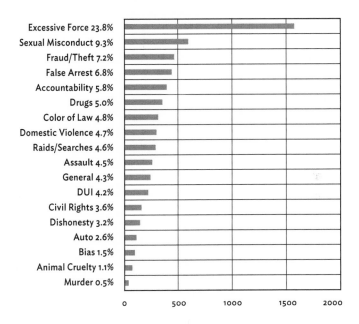

PROSECUTING POLICE MISCONDUCT

Per a recent analysis published this year, using data gathered by the NPMSRP from April 2009 through December 2010, it was determined that prosecuting police misconduct in the United States is very problematic, with conviction rates, incarceration rates, and the amount of time law enforcement officers spent behind bars for criminal misconduct all far less then what happens when ordinary citizens face criminal charges.

MISCONDUCT BY TYPE

Of the 6,613 law enforcement officers involved in reported allegations of misconduct that met NPMSRP criteria for tracking purposes, 1,575 were involved in excessive force reports, which were the most prominent type of reports at 23.8 percent of all reports. This was followed by sexual misconduct complaints at 9.3 percent of officers reported; then theft, fraud, and robbery allegations, involving 7.2 percent of all officers reported.

ACCORDING TO 2010 DATA

Approximately 11 percent of the officers' reports tracked that year involved U.S. drug policies.

Six hundred ninety-eight law enforcement officers were involved in reported misconduct that involved drugs in some way.

Three hundred forty-three of those law enforcement officers were criminally charged, convicted, or sentenced for those incidents.

At least seven lives were lost due to misconduct involving drug laws.

At least $11.2 million was spent in civil litigation due to drug law related police misconduct.

SUMMARY

From January 2010 through December 2010 the National Police Misconduct Statistics and Reporting Project recorded

4,861 unique reports of police conduct that involve 6,613 sworn law enforcement officers and 6,826 alleged victims.

4,861: unique reports of police misconduct tracked

6,613: number of sworn law enforcement officers, of which 354 were agency leaders such as Chiefs or Sheriffs.

6,826: number of alleged victims involved

247: number of fatalities associated with tracked reports

$346,512,800: estimated amount spent on misconduct related civil judgments and settlements, excluding sealed settlements, court costs, and attorney fees.

The NPMSRP utilizes the only consistent source of data available for police misconduct information since most states currently have laws that prevent the examination of police misconduct information recorded by individual agencies themselves by the public, and no other agency tracks police misconduct data in any publicly available way. Therefore, the NPMSRP must rely on media reports of police misconduct in order to gather data for statistical and trending analysis.

IGNORANCE OF THE LAW IS NO EXCUSE

What are Miranda rights?

In 1966, the U.S. Supreme Court decided the momentous case of *Miranda v. Arizona*, declaring that whenever a person is taken into police custody, before being questioned he or she must be told of the Fifth Amendment right not to make any self- incriminating statements. Thus, the Miranda rights were born.

Miranda warning

1. You have the right to remain silent.
2. Anything you say can and will be used against you in a court of law.
3. You have the right to talk to an attorney and have him/her present with you while you are being questioned.
4. If you cannot afford to hire an attorney, one will be appointed to represent you before any questions, if you wish.
5. You can decide at any time to exercise these rights and not answer any questions or make any statements.

Waiver

Do you understand each of these rights I have explained to you? Having these rights in mind, do you wish to talk to us now?

If you believe that your Miranda rights have been violated, this can have a significant impact on your case and may even lead to a dismissal of any charges against you.

CHAPTER 4

BIASED POLICING 101

To understand the history of the relationship between people of color and the police we first must look at four primary areas.

Fugitive Slave Act

A law passed as part of the Compromise of 1850, which provided Southern slaveholders with legal weapons to capture **slaves** who had escaped to the free states.

Slave catchers

Fugitive slave catchers were people who returned escaped slaves to their owners in the United States in the mid-nineteenth century.

White Supremacy

The belief that white people are superior to those of all other races, especially the black race, and should therefore dominate society.

Machiavellian

Italian diplomat Niccolo Machiavelli is best celebrated for writing *The Prince,* a handbook for unscrupulous politicians that inspired the term Machiavellian. This handbook for politicians on the use of ruthless, self-serving cunning established Machiavelli as the father of modern political theory.

Quotes from Machiavelli:

It is better to be feared than loved, if you cannot be both.

If an injury has to be done to a man it should be so severe that his vengeance need not be feared.

The first method for estimating the intelligence of a ruler
is to look at the men he has around him.

Some police departments in the early 1900s began to use the Machiavellian theory as a method to control the citizens in their jurisdictions. They also believed that respect was not necessary. Using fear to control the citizens was the best way to quickly gain compliance.

The FBI completed a thorough review of the KKK and white supremacy organizations that have infiltrated police departments. This report was dated 2006 and is readily available for review. It should be noted that the U.S. government began investigating white supremacy organizations in the early 1900s.

It should be observed that the evolution of the slave catcher to the earliest law enforcement officers demonstrates a pattern of behavior that has been devastating to people of color. Slave patrols and Night Watches, which later became modern police departments, were both designed to control the behaviors of minorities.

LADY JUSTICE

Lady Justice is a symbol whose attributes I, as a police instructor, make sure all officers are aware of. I believe that if police officers use the concept of Lady Justice to evaluate

23

their behavior there would be fewer problems both for them as well as for the citizens.

Her blindfold stands for:

Judgments of objectivity and/or dispassionate decisions or conclusions not manipulated by wealth, politics, or popularity. Justice should be rendered without passion or prejudice.

The sword she holds stands for:

The enforcement extent of Lady Justice. It means she stands prepared to compel truthfulness to her decision of purpose and justice by both parties. She does not control by fisted threat or terror or use of a weapon but instead she rules and openly exhibits that she is prepared to get respect. Justice can be swift and final.

The scale she holds in her hand stand for:

The fact that Lady Justice judiciously weighs the claims of each side. They are revealed as the scales of justice. Each scale presents a measure of evidence. Lady Justice weighs the aspects of a case to render a decision.

CHAPTER 5

RACIALLY & CULTURALLY BIASED POLICING

Racial profiling is defined as the practice by which police officers stop motorists of certain racial and ethnic groups because the officers believe that these groups are more likely than others to commit certain types of crimes.

Racially and culturally biased policing occurs when law enforcement inappropriately considers race, ethnicity, or culture in deciding with whom and how to intervene in an enforcement capacity.

The fundamental goal of understanding racially and culturally biased policing is to expose, examine, and discuss the pattern of behavior that officers exhibit when they engage in racially and culturally biased policing. The proper methods for stopping and approaching vehicles as well as police contacts are very important to the day-to-day operation of today's police officers.

If I like a person—if I think they contribute to society and I value them as a person—quite likely I would treat them a certain way. If I don't like a person—if I feel they do not contribute to society and I don't value them as a human being—most likely I will treat them a certain way.

A bias, whether it be positive or negative, exhibits a certain pattern of behavior. This is especially true when a police officer carries such a bias with them into the day-to-day role in which they serve our society.

As a police officer, you must keep your biases to yourself and treat each person fairly, equally, and with respect. Each person is to be treated fairly under the law.

Police officers, as they perform their operational duty, must always ask and take into account the following considerations:

What is the legal justification required to make this vehicle stop?

Recognize the consideration for selecting the best communication options for this police contact.

List the types of information the officer should provide the dispatcher before getting out of the police car.

Explain why racial profiling is not allowed.

Demonstrate the skills needed to recognize racial profiling.

Examine the term "pretextual stop" from a legal viewpoint.

Explain how racially and culturally biased policing can erode the trust between the police department and the community.

Articulate the situations when race or other conditions justify a lawful police encounter.

During my travels as a police trainer I have encountered numerous officers who believe that people of color are genetically predisposed to be criminals. As a police officer, if I truly believe this, the way I would engage these individuals would certainly be different from those who I believed were not predisposed to be criminals.

Police work is inherently a dangerous profession. Those who choose this career must have a passion for it. I tell people all the time that whenever you must swear an oath to a profession you must truly be dedicated. Not all careers are for all people.

For police officers to be effective and follow the letter of the law, there must be certain guidelines in place. When a police officer stops a vehicle for a traffic stop there is a certain basic operational procedure that must be followed. Although states vary in the specifics of the types of enforcement actions police officers can conduct, these are some of the basic operational guidelines:

Each time a police officer stops the driver of a motor vehicle for a violation of any motor vehicle statute or ordinance, that officer shall report the following information to the law enforcement agency that employs the officer:

A.   The age, gender, and race or minority group of the individual stopped

B.   The traffic violation or violations alleged to have been committed that led to the stop

C.   Whether a search was conducted because of the stop

D.   If a search was conducted, did the individual consent to the search? Was there probable cause for the search? Was the person's property searched? What was the duration of the search?

E.   Whether any contraband was discovered during the search and the type of any contraband discovered

F.   Whether any warning or citation was issued because of the stop

G.   If a warning or citation was issued, the violation charge or warning provided

H.   Whether an arrest was made because of either the stop or the search

I.   If an arrest was made, the crime charged

J.   The location of the stop

As you can see there are numerous procedures and protocols that today's law enforcement officer must follow to not only be effective but to work within the guidelines of the law. At the end of the day, officer safety is paramount for the officer's survival.

SAMPLE LAW ENFORCEMENT BIAS-BASED PROFILING POLICY

Purpose

The purpose of this general order is to state unequivocally that law enforcement activities that are the result of bias-based profiling are not condoned, are unacceptable, and will not be tolerated by the police department. Bias-based profiling is unethical and illegal, and serves to foster distrust of law enforcement by the community we serve. This order will serve as a guideline for police officers to prevent such occurrences and to protect our personnel, when they act within the provisions of the law and this order, from unwarranted accusations. This general order confirms to all federal mandates and revised Missouri statutes 590.650, and 590.050, associated with encounters between police officers and citizens during traffic arrest, traffic stops, and investigative detentions.

Definitions

A. Bias-based profiling commonly referred to as racial profiling is the selection of individuals based solely on a trait common to a group for enforcement action. This includes, but is not limited to, race, ethnic background, gender, sexual orientation, religion, economic status, age, cultural group, or any other identifiable group.

B. Enforcement activities both on and off duty, undertaken by police department personnel that arise from their

authority related to employment, oath of office, state
statute, or federal law. Activities such as traffic contacts,
field contacts, arrests, investigations, asset seizures, and
forfeitures, and general law enforcement contact with
citizens.

C. Reasonable suspicion that is more than a mere hunch, but
is based on a set of articulable facts and circumstances
that would warn a person of reasonable caution in believ-
ing that a violation of the law had been committed, is
about to be committed, or is in the process of being committed, by the person or persons under suspicion. This
information can be based on observations, training and
experience, or reliable information received from credible
outside sources.

Policy

A. The police department respects and protects the rights of
every individual and pledges to treat everyone fairly and
without favoritism in all enforcement actions.

B. All investigative detention traffic stops, arrests, searches
and seizures of property, including asset seizure and forfeiture efforts, by commissioned police personnel will be
based on standards of reasonable suspicion or probable
cause as required by the Fourth Amendment of the U.S.
Constitution and statutory authority.

C. All investigative detentions, traffic stops, arrests, searches or seizures of property, including asset seizure and forfeiture efforts, based on race, ethnicity, gender, sexual orientation, religious beliefs, disability, handicap or health-related conditions, or economic level conducted without probable cause or reasonable suspicion, are strictly forbidden. Officers must be able to articulate specific facts, circumstances, and conclusions that support probable cause or reasonable suspicion for the arrest, traffic stop, or investigative detention.

D. Proactive traffic enforcement and stops are an effective and important law enforcement function. Enforcement efforts are critical in saving lives and reducing injuries that are attributed to either drunk driving or individuals that wantonly violate the traffic laws of our state and communities. In addition, traffic law enforcement is an effective tool in gathering evidence, apprehending fugitives and combating illegal drugs, illegal weapons, and other criminal activity.

E. The police department general order manual, that has been made available to all employees in both written and electronic form, identifies specific procedures to be used during investigative detentions, traffic stops, use of force, and search and seizures.

F. The police department will investigate all complaints of bias-based profiling and will conduct an annual

administrative review of statistical traffic, field interview, and asset forfeiture data to determine and verify
compliance.

G. Corrective measures will be taken to remedy any violation of this policy. Corrective measures may include,
but are not limited to, training, counseling, policy
review, and discipline up to and including termination
of employment.

H. All sworn officers shall receive annual bias-based profiling related training. This training will be conducted and
documented by supervisors at the platoon level. Training
documentation will be forwarded to the professional
standards office. This training may include the viewing
of video tapes, web-based computer courses, or policy
review and legal updates related to bias-based profiling
and is a requirement of the Missouri law enforcement
continuing education requirement.

**The preceding was excerpted from the Kinloch Police
Department Bias-Based Profiling Policy**

THE ESCALATION OF FORCE INDEX
AND FORCE CONTINUUMS

Force continuums are guides that police departments use to define the actions of the police officer as well as the actions of the subject. These force continuums vary by name and scope but are designed to identify the behaviors and actions of both the police officer and the subject.

Force continuums also look at escalation and de-escalation of force as a sliding scale that is ultimately determined by the officer's perception.

The escalation of force index was constructed to give law enforcement officers a guide to follow when interpreting the subject's resistive behavior, and the appropriate response to this behavior. This information is only a guide and by no means replaces the officer's judgment relative to an assault on his or her safety. When faced with potentially violent encounters, the officer must always be aware of:

- appropriate control techniques;
- his/her basic fighting skills; and
- level of personal physical conditioning

Officers are permitted to use the amount of physical force reasonable and necessary to impose custody and overcome all resistance; and also to ensure the safety of the officer, arrested subject, and others in the vicinity of the arrest.

A. Conflict escalation (those actions of the subject)

1. MENACE PHASE

   Definition—threats and perceived intimidation through nonverbal mannerisms

2. AGITATOR PHASE

   Definition—attempts to disturb or excite through verbal dialogue

3. PASSIVE PHASE

   Definition—nonresistant inaction with the intent to prevent officer's control

4. DEFIANCE PHASE

   Definition—nonsubmissive acts to prevent officer from controlling the subject, although not to injure officer

5. FORMIDABLE DYNAMIC PHASE

   Definition—bodily actions of attack with intent to injure officer

6. VIRULENT PHASE

   Definition—lethal force occurrence

B. Conflict resolution (those actions of the officer)

1. COMMAND PRESENCE

   Definition—immediate recognition of control

2. COMMAND DIALOGUE

   Definition- verbalization relative to custody or control

3. UNARMED CONTROL

   (a) minimum force unarmed control

Definition—procedures where the possibility of subject injury is slight

(b) maximum force unarmed control

Definition—procedures where the possibility of subject injury is common

4. INTERMEDIARY WEAPONS

(a) MINIMUM force intermediary weapon control

Definition—baton control holds

(b) MAXIMUM force intermediary weapon control

Definition—baton strikes

5. DEADLY FORCE

Definition—causing or likely to cause death

C. Escalation of force index variables

The following variables may affect an officer's decision in escalating or deescalating the level of control

1. OFFICER/ SUBJECT SIZE

2. ENVIRONMENTAL CONDITIONS/ TOTALITY OF CIRCUMSTANCES

3. REACTION TIME

D. Principles of controlling resistive behavior

Generally, all subject control techniques utilize one of these principles to control resistive behavior.

1. PAIN COMPLIANCE

Definition—the use of the stimulus of pain to control resistive behavior

2. STUNNING

   Definition—stimulation of overwhelming sensory input

3. DISTRACTION TECHNIQUE

   Definition—control techniques that weaken motor
   action by changing the thought process

4. BALANCE DISPLACEMENT

   Definition—control techniques that displace
   balance through principles of leverage

5. MOTOR DYSFUNCTIONS

   Definition—controlled striking techniques which
   overstimulate motor nerves, causing temporary
   muscle impairment

SAMPLE LAW ENFORCEMENT DEPARTMENT USE OF FORCE CONTINUUM

Purpose

The purpose of this general order is to establish policy and procedure for the use of lethal and less lethal force by members of this department. The order is for department use only and does not apply in any criminal or civil proceedings. This order should not be construed as a creation of a higher legal standard of safety or care in an evidentiary sense with respected third-party claims.

This order will only form the basis for departmental administrative review and possible corrective action concerning conduct allegedly performed without regard for the guidance and policy, although this conduct may conform to all legal norms of care and safety.

Policy

The department recognizes and respects the value and special integrity of each human life. Investing police officers with the lawful authority to use force to protect the public welfare, a careful balancing of all human interest is required. Officers are confronted with situations where control must be exercised to affect the rest and to protect the public safety. Control may be achieved verbally through instruction, advice, warnings, and persuasions, or by the use of physical force.

While the use of reasonable physical force may be necessary in certain situations, it cannot be of unreasonable control. Force may not be resorted to unless all the other reasonable alternatives have been exhausted and must clearly be ineffective under a particular set of circumstances. Therefore, it is the policy of this department that police officers use only that force that appears reasonably necessary to effectively bring the incident under control or prevent unlawful behavior and accomplish lawful objectives, while protecting the lives and safety of the officer or another. Verbal or physical abuse is forbidden.

An officer may use lethal force only when the officer reasonably believes that the action is in defense of human life, including the officer's own life, or in defense of any person in imminent danger or serious physical injury. A police officer must weigh the necessity of apprehension against the apparent threat to the safety of all involved, and exhaust every alternative means of apprehension known to be available at the time before resorting to the use of lethal force. Lethal force will not be used if it is a clear risk to the safety of a third person, even if no other means exist for apprehension.

Definitions

A. Excessive force—all force beyond what is reasonably required for self-defense, or to take a person into custody

B. Firearms—any weapon from which a projectile is forcibly ejected by an explosive not to include the advanced Taser electronic incapacitation device

C. Lethal force—that force which is likely to cause death or serious physical injury

D. Less lethal force—that is less than lethal force

E. Lethal weapon—any weapon that is likely to cause death when properly used according to training

F. Less lethal weapon—a weapon not likely to cause death when properly used according to training

G. Officer—a sworn officer having a Class A POST license to include reserves

H. Reasonable belief—a logical, articulable conclusion drawn from facts and circumstances which would be evident to a person of average intelligence and intellect

l.   Serious physical injury—an injury that creates a sub-
      stantial risk of death or that causes severe disfigurement
      or protracted loss or impairment of the function of any
      body part

**Excerpted from the Kinloch Police Department Use of
Force Policy.**

CHAPTER 6

REASONABLE ALTERNATIVES TO THE USE OF DEADLY FORCE

Reasonable alternatives to the use of deadly force were developed to reduce the number of police-related shootings. This process is accomplished by providing the officer a multitude of alternatives to assist in the decision-making process. These reasonable alternatives are defined as time, use of cover, verbal commands, calling for assistance, backup element, use of pepper spray (oleoresin capsicum), use of the baton or other impact weapon, use of tactical retreat, tactical element, defensive tactics skills, and use of the Taser. Each of these alternatives is based on the totality of the circumstances.

Each person realizes that police work has a certain element of danger built into the profession. Each situation the officer finds himself in has the potential to become a deadly force situation. If an officer fears for his life or fears he's in reasonable danger or has a fear of serious physical injury or death, most departments acknowledge that deadly force is one option.

We must also consider that if there are options other than deadly force is it reasonable for the officer to attempt these alternatives. Only the officer at the moment of truth can decide if these options are reasonable. No one expects an officer to put their head into a lion's mouth; however, a professional police officer must weigh all options and determine which one is the most valid.

Every officer must be able to determine which force options are best used. The officer must be able to define each of the reasonable alternatives to the use of deadly force. Each officer must determine appropriate factors when deciding which reasonable alternatives to use. Respectively, the officer must identify the legal justification required prior to an officer using deadly force. Individually the officer must explain why being in fear of his life is no longer the only standard for using deadly force.

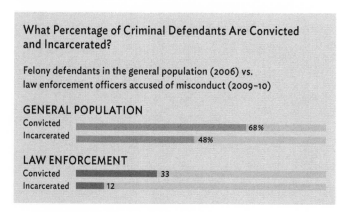

What Percentage of Criminal Defendants Are Convicted and Incarcerated?

Felony defendants in the general population (2006) vs. law enforcement officers accused of misconduct (2009–10)

GENERAL POPULATION

Convicted	68%
Incarcerated	48%

LAW ENFORCEMENT

Convicted	33
Incarcerated	12

Reasonable alternatives concept

The concept of reasonable alternatives was developed to give the officer an opportunity to escalate or de-escalate the level of force used relative to the nature of the situation prior to deadly force.

Definition of basic reasonable alternatives

The first basic reasonable alternative to the use of deadly force is time. As an asset to the officer, the use of time can be utilized by certain actions and decisions made by the officer to increase in scope as to give the officer more options and control.

Next is the use of cover: any object that would deflect a projectile such as a bullet can be used by the officer for his or her safety in a confrontation.

Verbal commands are requests, advice, persuasion, orders, and warnings all coupled with tactical communication and a strong command presence. These techniques can diffuse a hostile situation prior to the use of physical force.

Calling for assistance is the use of the dispatcher as an aid in creating a more controlled procedure for capturing the subject while minimizing the potential risk of injury to the officer.

Backup element is the use of backup to create a more effective means of control by adding the additional cover officers and control for the primary officer.

Use of pepper mace products containing oleoresin capsicum are highly effective on individuals under the influence of alcohol or drugs, and persons with mental or emotional problems. This product incapacitates immediately and does no permanent physical harm.

The use of the baton or impact weapon such as nightstick is used as an intermediary weapon to cause a temporary motor dysfunction in the subject. It is used on the legs. The intent is to end violent aggression against the officer without serious physical injury to the subject.

Many officers are hesitant to use tactical retreat measures. When faced with a potentially dangerous situation, the officer can disengage from the subject to regroup to a more tactically sound procedure. We must also keep in mind that in any physical encounter with an officer and subject the officer always has two options: penetrate or disengage. All too often officers focus on escalation procedures and only rarely on deescalation procedures.

Tactical elements are specialized units within the police department that can be brought into a situation to resolve it effectively. This would include divisions such as hostage response units, canine units, mobile reserve units, SWAT units, etc.

Defensive tactics skills, which include various methods for overcoming a multitude of resistive situations, can be implemented with the use of defensive tactics techniques. These techniques include but are not limited to joint locks, pressure point control, countermeasures, ground fighting, and carotid neck restraint. All these techniques can be used to control the subject.

REASONABLE ALTERNATIVES TO THE USE OF DEADLY FORCE

To be effective today's trained police officer must keep his skill sets in defensive tactics ready at all times. Most police departments spend a considerable amount of time conducting training for officers in firearms. Some departments mandate that their officers qualify in the use of their firearms two to six times per year. While many officers go their entire career without ever having to discharge their weapon at a subject, most police officers at some time in their career are going to have to handcuff a subject, escort that subject away from a crime scene, or physically engage that subject in some type of hand-to-hand combat situation. Although constant training in firearms is certainly a good idea, it should not exclude training in defensive tactics.

The officer determines the appropriate factors when deciding which reasonable alternatives to utilize.

The primary goal of reasonable alternatives to the use of deadly force include subject control with the officer using only that force that is reasonable and necessary. The officer is better able to determine the appropriate threat level and the force option. The officer utilizes the reaction time range principle, and he or she utilizes the reactionary gap.

Reaction time is defined as the amount of time required between observing an act and the individual's reaction or response to that act. In police training we often see that as approximately half a second.

In police training we generally identify approximately six feet as the reactionary gap. The reactionary gap is a safety zone between the officer and the offender that affords the officer more time to react to aggression:

A. average distance is six feet
B. varies with the type of weapon offender possesses
    (Reactionary options to resistance)
C. penetrate the gap to attempt control techniques
D. disengage to increase space

To reinforce the protocols and procedures to be used when deciding force options, training scenarios can be used that depict right way and better way processes the officer can observe and practice. When an officer uses force options that are not reasonable, the outcomes can be observed and debriefed. When an officer utilizes appropriate responses to force options, the positive options are also observed and discussed.

Identify the legal justification required prior to an officer using deadly force. Most police departments reinforce the theory that if an officer is in fear of serious injury or death, then deadly force is justified. The idea that the use of deadly force is both *reasonable* and *necessary* remains a relatively new concept police departments are introducing into their training curriculums.

As a training method to teach officers the skills to determine which levels of force to use when faced with a deadly force situation, I wholeheartedly recommend multimedia training presentations or videos that look at the different types of force options and how the outcomes can vary. Each video presented is designed to reinforce positive outcomes to responding to a variety of calls. The types of calls observed could include flourishing, disturbances, holdup in progress, traffic stop, robberies, and citizen contacts.

Let's take a look at some of the news stories that generated national outrage regarding the deaths of unarmed black males. On Staten Island, New York, the July 2014 death of Eric Gardner caused by what appeared to be a chokehold by a New York City officer created outrage within the community. August 2014 in Ferguson, Missouri, a predominantly black community, the shooting death of Michael Brown by officer Darren Wilson, a white officer, generated not only local but national protests and furthered a discussion about whether black citizens are treated fairly at the hands of the police. In Cleveland, Ohio, a twelve-year-old black male, identified as Tamir Rice, while playing in the park with a toy gun, was shot and killed by an officer of the Cleveland Police Department. Walter L. Scott was shot by a police officer in North Charleston, South Carolina, during a traffic stop. Although this officer denied any wrongdoing, a subsequent video proved otherwise. In 2015 Freddie Gray died while in police custody in Baltimore, Maryland. In the Freddie Gray case it should be noted that his injuries apparently were sustained during his transportation from the scene to the police department. Each of these incidents generated widespread unrest and often civil disobedience. A 2014 Pew Research Center survey confirms stark racial divisions in response to the Ferguson police shooting. FBI director James B. Comey stated in a speech he gave during February 2015 that "demographic data regarding officer-involved shootings is not consistently reported to us through our uniform crime reporting program. Because reporting is voluntary, our data is incomplete and therefore in the aggregate unreliable."

In October 2014, an article by *ProPublica*, an investigative outlet, concluded that young black males are twenty-one times more likely to be shot by police than their white counterparts.

DEFINITION OF BASIC "REASONABLE ALTERNATIVES"

Reasonable Alternatives

- The concept of "reasonable alternatives" was developed to give officers an opportunity to escalate or deescalate the level of force used relative to the nature of the situation prior to deadly force.

  • TIME • USE OF COVER • VERBAL COMMANDS • CALLING FOR ASSISTANCE • BACKUP ELEMENT • USE OF PEPPER MACE, ETC.

TIME

- As an asset to the officer the use of time can be utilized by certain actions and decisions made by the officer to increase in scope as to give the officer more options and control.

Use of Cover

- Any object that will deflect a projectile, (e.g., "a bullet"), can be used by the officer for his or her safety in a confrontation.

Verbal Commands

- Making requests, advising, persuasion, orders, and warnings all coupled with tactical communication, and a strong command presence can diffuse a hostile situation prior to the use of physical force.

Calling for Assistance

- The use of the dispatcher as an aid in a more controlled procedure for capturing a subject can be established while minimizing the potential risk of injury to the officer.

Backup Element

- The use of backup creates a more effective means of control by adding the additional cover officers and control for the primary officer(s).

Use of OC

- Products containing oleoresin capsicum are highly effective on individuals under the influence of alcohol or drugs, and persons with mental or emotional problems.

Use of Baton

- The impact weapon (nightstick) when used as an intermediary weapon causes a temporary motor dysfunction in the subject's arms or legs thus ending violent aggression against the officer without serious physical injury to the subject.

Tactical Retreat

- When faced with a potentially dangerous situation the officer can disengage from the subject to regroup to a more tactically sound procedure.

Tactical Element

- Specialized units within the police department can be brought into a situation to resolve it effectively; (e.g., hostage response unit, canine unit, SWAT unit, etc.)

Defensive Tactics Skills

- Various methods for overcoming a multitude of resistive situations can be implemented with the use of DT skills. Joint locks, pressure points, countermeasures, and ground fighting are but a few of the techniques that the trained police officer can use in controlling a subject.

TASER

- The Taser has been used by police departments around the country to control subjects while minimizing injury.

Excessive Force by Type

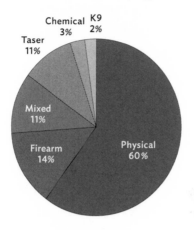

DEADLY FORCE

Deadly force is an amount of force that is likely to cause either serious bodily injury or death to another person.

Police officers may use deadly force in specific circumstances when they are trying to enforce the law.

Private citizens may use deadly force in certain circumstances in self-defense. For police officers, the rules governing the use of deadly force are different from those for citizens.

For deadly force to be constitutional when an arrest is taking place, it must be the reasonable choice under all the circumstances at the time. Therefore, deadly force should be looked at as an option that is used when it is believed that no other action will succeed. The model Penal Code, although not adopted in all states, restricts police actions regarding deadly force. According to the code, officers should not use deadly force unless the action would not endanger innocent bystanders, the suspect used deadly force in committing the crime, or the officer believes a delay in arrest may result in injury or death to other people.

The statutory principles allow an officer to use lethal physical force when the officer reasonably believes it is necessary to defend himself or herself or a third person when the use or eminent use of lethal physical force to arrest or prevent the escape of someone the officer reasonably considers has committed or attempted to commit a felony concerning the infliction or threat of serious physical injury or death and, if feasible, the officer has given notice to his or her intent to use lethal physical force.

STATUTORY STANDARDS FOR USING
DEADLY PHYSICAL FORCE

The law allows law enforcement officers to use deadly physical force only when they are reasonably believed it to be necessary to:

- protect themselves or a third person from the use or eminent use of physical deadly force; or
- make an arrest or avert the escape from custody of an individual who they reasonably believe has committed or endeavored to commit a felony involving the infliction or

threatened infliction or grave physical injury and, where feasible, they have specified warnings of their intent to use deadly physical force.

The law defines deadly physical force as physical force that can be logically expected to cause death or serious physical injury. It describes serious physical injury as physical injury which produces a substantial risk of death or which causes serious disfigurement, serious impairment of health, or serious harm or impairment of the function of any bodily organ.

The law specifies that a reasonable certainty that an individual has committed an offense means a reasonable belief in actualities or circumstances which, if true, would constitute an offense. If the alleged facts or circumstances would not establish an offense and erroneous, though not unjustifiable, acceptance that the law is otherwise does not make the use of physical force justifiable to make an arrest or to prevent an escape from custody.

Why an Officer Being in Fear if His or Her Life Is No Longer the Only Standard for Using Deadly Force

For an officer's actions to be considered justifiable when deciding to use deadly force the officer must ask this question: Do I have any other reasonable options to the use of deadly force that can be applied in this situation? For deadly force to be justified the officer's actions must not only be reasonable but must also be necessary. When officers find themselves in a rapidly escalating situation, they may believe they are in fear for their life or serious physical injury. At this junction, some officers believe that the only option is the use of deadly force. The decision to use deadly force is going to be driven by what is known as *a totality of the circumstances.*

TOTALITY OF THE CIRCUMSTANCES

The totality of the circumstances standard proposes that there is no solitary deciding aspect, that one must consider all the facts, the context, and determine from the whole picture whether there is probable cause. In addition, it must be determined whether an anticipated detention is really a detention, or whether an officer acted under color of law. The chief guide for this kind of substantial rule is the feature patterns from cases in which the courts have found the criteria were met.

THE BROKEN OFFICER

It is certainly noteworthy that in many departments officers are suffering from various stages of mental health issues. In some departments, traditionally, some officers refuse to discuss any type of mental health issue since they believe it is a sign of weakness. These officers report for duty wearing a mask to hide their inner feelings and emotional frustrations. Sometimes these issues are psychological or emotional in nature and may manifest in various ways during their tour of duty.

If officers have witnessed numerous traumatic circumstances during their career as a police officer often these situations will become evident in ways that impact the officers' performance. We must not forget that police officers are human. Some officers truly believe they have an "S" for Superman on their chests and as such are immune to mental health issues that can affect anyone at any time. There must be a mechanism in place to evaluate an officer's mental health as well as their readiness for duty. If not, we are creating numerous ticking time bombs that can explode at any minute and impact the community in ways that would truly be devastating and counterproductive.

Each day police departments work to provide officers the training they need to recognize mental health issues among the populations that they serve. However, how often do these same departments provide mental health assessments for these very same officers, especially when they recognize these officers are suffering from some type of mental health issue?

Police work is stressful work. Working in an environment filled with danger, misery, and constant safety issues puts officers in a very high-stress career. When officers become psychologically unbalanced, the immune system becomes compromised as well. Stress can have a variety of impacts on the human body, and as police officers well know each day is filled with various levels of stressors. Often female police officers feel more stress than their male counterparts. It's still basically a male occupation and often female officers feel isolated on the job. Intervention should be mandated by police departments for their police officers to deal with this stressful profession.

Police suicide is also an issue that departments must come to terms with. Departments must not wait for officers to be in crisis or suicidal before they take a proactive approach. For each officer that contemplates suicide there are a vast number of officers out there working and suffering from the symptoms of posttraumatic stress disorder (PTSD).

In my career as a police officer I have known several officers who have committed suicide. The surviving officers often feel that their colleagues who took their lives are somehow weak or did not possess the internal fortitude to handle the job. There is a stigma among officers that if they should die on the job it should be in some type of blaze of glory such as rescuing someone from a burning building or running into a hail of gunfire during a bank robbery. All too often, when asked, officers will say that when another officer takes his or her life, this is in some way a sign of weakness

It is my hope that police departments will put in place some type of early warning system or evaluation process that they can use to assess an officer's mental well-being each year and determine if that officer is truly fit for duty.

EAP

After a shooting, many officers show symptoms of posttraumatic stress disorder. They may embrace increased alcohol use, have nightmares about faulty guns, experience physical illness, develop an incapacity to sleep or hold down food, and go through the stages of self-doubt, depression, anger, and guilt. A common symptom is ruminating or brooding about the shooting. Even if officers do not draw or fire their guns during a terrifying confrontation, they may experience symptoms of postshooting trauma. Untreated, postshooting trauma could ultimately develop into PTSD.

Employee assistance programs (EAPs) are voluntary, work-based programs that advance free and private assessments, short-term counseling, referrals, and follow-up services to personnel who have personal and/or work-related PROBLEMS. EAP addresses a wide-ranging and complex body of issues affecting mental and emotional well-being, such as alcohol and other substance abuse, stress, grief, family problems, and psychological disorders. EAP counselors also service in consultative roles with managers and supervisors to report employees and organize organizational trials and needs. Employee assistance programs or EAP are active in aiding organizations in preventing and managing workplace violence, trauma, and additional emergency response situations. Sometimes these programs are called police employment assistance programs or PEAP.

BREATHING AND MEDITATION

As police officers face the stress and frustration of performing their duty it is important for them to have access to activities that can help reduce their stress level and put them into a more favorable disposition. It should be noted that meditation and breathing techniques for over thousands of years have been used by many individuals around the world to help relax them as well as reduce their stress level and give them a sense of peace.

In my youth, I was very interested in martial arts. One of the first martial arts I studied was Aikido, which focuses on using your opponent's strength and energy against them. In addition, breathing and meditation is a core component of Aikido known as Ki development. Ki *a.k.a.* Chi or vital energy is cultivated on a daily basis. Ki is a universal energy source that flows through the body as well as outside it. As I developed my skills in Aikido, which is known as a soft style, I also learned and started to practice harder styles of martial arts such as Muay Thai and Jujitsu.

It has been my experience that both meditation and breathing flow from the same spring. As one seeks to delve deeper into meditation, breathing becomes an intricate part of that process. The first stage of meditation is to stop distractions, clear one's mind, and relax as deeply as possible. It is important to choose a peaceful and quiet place to begin the meditation process. Whether you meditate first thing in the morning or at the end of your day, one of the most important things is to be consistent. Those individuals who begin their day and end their day with meditation see positive benefits.

As we begin the breathing process there are several variations that one can choose. For me one of the most basic breathing techniques is to first place yourself in a relaxed position either sitting on the floor or even in a chair. Now breathe deeply, and as much as you can, hold the breath as long as you can, then breathe out, emptying the lungs as fully as possible. Start doing this in five-minute intervals beginning with your first session at three to five minutes. When you can work up to maintaining this process for fifteen to thirty minutes, this is a very good start.

While breathing deeply and exhaling deeply completely or partially, close your eyes, clear your mind, and think positive thoughts. Some envision themselves on a beach, others in a forest; but it is more important to be in a peaceful environment within your mind. There will be a great temptation to follow the different thoughts as they arise within your mind but attempt to remain focused and keep your goal on the sensation of your breath in addition to the peaceful state you find yourself in.

If we practice consistently in this way, our distractions will subside and we will experience a sense of inner peace, relaxation, and a certain sense of tranquility. Even though this type of breathing meditation is only a preliminary stage, it can be quite powerful and revitalizing. From this process, we seek inner peace and an opportunity to control our mind and reduce our stress level without being dependent on external forces.

There are many different types of meditation one can seek, such as transcendental meditation, which will help the individual to pursue their goal of peace and tranquility even further. Some seek out yoga as a method of meditation and exercise; this also has tremendous value. As a police officer, regardless of whether you seek personal meditation and breathing, yoga, transcendental meditation, or some other variation, as long as you are seeking to calm your mind and reduce your stress level, at the end of the day you will be most successful.

When we have settled down comfortably and begun our meditation process, we gently turn our attention to our breath, always letting it focus as a rhythm and remain normal. As we breathe out we imagine that we are breathing away all the negative forces within us. As we breathe in we imagine we are breathing in positivity, hope, and a certain measure of stress reduction through peace and inner tranquility. Many of these breathing techniques can be done at any time when you feel the need to reduce your stress level.

CHAPTER 7

SCENARIO-BASED TRAINING

In the world of training, one of the most effective methods I have seen revolves around experiential learning as well as scenario-based training. The following are a few methods that involve this type of training as it helps the officer to further understand their strengths and limitations as well as gives them an opportunity to debrief afterward to find better methods to improve their performance.

Scenario-based training can be conducted in one room, an entire building, or multiple buildings. The use of citizens as role players also adds an additional amount of realism to this training and engages the citizens to understand more about what police officers do as they perform their duty. I have had great success using high school students, theater students, as well as members of churches and community groups. To keep a safe environment, only prop-type weapons are used at the scene. The role players are given specific instructions and are told not to deviate from them to keep this scenario-based training realistic. Evaluators are on site to control the scenes as well as evaluate the officers' performance. At the completion of the training a debrief is held so that the officers can learn what they did well in addition to areas where improvement is needed. I encourage videotaping all the role-playing scenarios to better guide the officers during debrief so that they can actually see what occurred and determine how to improve their performance as well as the skill sets they used that were appropriate.

Scenario-based training at its most rudimentary level looks at the tactically incorrect way and improved or tactically correct way as opposed to the wrong way.

The following are several different types of presentations that can either be constructed as actual on-site scenario-based training or can be reproduced in videos that officers can review and comment on afterward.

Two additional forms of police-based training include nonlethal simunition training and use of force simulators. Each of these training systems adds an additional amount of realism to improve performance.

Flourishing call

In the first scenario, officers respond to a park on a call for flourishing. Upon arrival, they see a group of people arguing in the park as one subject attempts to leave. The officers engage the subject who is attempting to leave and ask him to stop. Without taking tactical precautions the officers approach the subject at which time he pulls out a firearm and shoots the officer in the chest. The second officer winds up shooting the subject thus ending the confrontation.

The first presentation looks at flourishing of a weapon.

Opening scene shows situation from a wrong-way perspective.

After showing wrong-way clip, discuss the negative or improper procedures utilized by the officers.

Encourage class feedback among the officers.

The opening scene of the second clip shows the situation from a more tactically sound perspective.

Upon completion of the second flourishing clip, discuss positive measures utilized by the officers.

Often this scenario reveals several specific issues. Officers, upon receiving the call, looked at it as a routine call. Officers failed to advise dispatcher of their arrival to call. Officers failed to take an impact weapon, and the second officer failed to backup his partner. His attention was on the victim not the subject.

The second time the officers engaged the subject in the scenario, they discussed the call prior to arrival. Officers advised the dispatcher of their arrival. Officers decided in advance who would be the contact officer and who would be the cover officer. Officers, upon arrival, evaluated the situation, took cover, and took a defensive position. Officers utilized sound tactics and officer safety procedures.

Here are some other scenarios that can be used:

Robbery call

Two officers respond to an apartment where they are met by a fifty-year-old male who informs them that while walking home from work three white males approached him at gunpoint and took his wallet. He further states he was not injured although the male with the weapon threatened him several times that he was going to shoot him. How the officers gather information relative to the suspects, last known location, witnesses at the scene, and officer safety will be observed. Information the officers relay to communications is critical. Note that there will be three role players at the scene who are potential witnesses.

SCENARIO-BASED TRAINING

Disturbance call

Two officers respond to a call for disturbance. Upon arrival, the officers enter the residence and observe two individuals, a male and female husband-and-wife, arguing. The husband is very loud, and argumentative while the female is crying. Note that they are presently in the kitchen of their residence. It should be noted that the officers are being evaluated on how they diffuse this conflict as well as their officer safety procedures. Observe that the individuals are in the kitchen and surrounded by a variety of knives and other instruments.

For safety, all the knives are fake. If the officers fail to control the situation or use poor officer safety tactics, the female will take one of the knives and attempt to stab her husband.

Traffic stop

This scene takes place outside and involves a police car and a regular motor vehicle. The vehicle is occupied by two to four males and loud music is playing. The officers stopped the vehicle for violating a stop sign. As the officers approach the vehicle, it should be noticed if they are using tactics that would ensure their safety as well as monitoring the behavior of the occupants in the vehicle. Prior to exiting the police vehicle, it should be observed if the officers contact the dispatcher and what type of information they give the dispatcher. What type of conversation do they have between each other prior to engaging the subjects in the vehicle? Did the officers decide who would be the contact officer? Were officer safety tactics applied?

If the officers use good tactics and communication skills all the occupants in the vehicle will cooperate. If the subjects in the vehicle see an opportunity to run, one of the subjects will exit the vehicle.

Fight in progress call

Two officers respond to an apartment on a call for a fight in progress. Upon arrival, they hear loud music and cursing and screaming coming from the apartment. As the officers approach the apartment it should be noted whether they are discussing the tactics they plan to apply and how they plan on making their approach. As one of the officers knocks on the door, suddenly the door opens and inside two female subjects are fighting in the rear. A white powdery substance is observed in plain view on a table. It should be mentioned how the officers enter the residence, if they observe the white powdery substance, and how they take control of the scene. If the officers fail to take control of the scene, two of the individuals will attempt to run from the residence as a means of escape. Do the officers call for backup? Do the officers place the subjects in control positions? Which tactics do the officers apply as they engage these individuals?

Call for a shooting

Two officers receive a call for a shooting. The location is the front outside area of a building. Upon arrival, they observe a male subject on the ground unconscious covered in blood. There are two to four individuals standing around the subject all claiming they did not see what happened. Upon interviewing the individuals, one of the officers determines that a subject ran from the scene approximately five minutes before their arrival. This individual is responsible for the shooting. It should be remarked how the officers interview the individuals, what type of information they gather, and if they maintain safety procedures during this incident. The information they forward to the dispatcher—(i.e., subject description, last known location, if armed, etc.)—will be under review.

Call for a rape

One officer responds to a call for a rape. Upon arrival, he or she is met by a female adult who tells the officer her thirteen-year-old daughter was raped by her boyfriend. It should be stated that the boyfriend is still at the residence. The officer's investigative skills, ability to control the scene, and render whatever type of aid to the victim is under observation. It should be further observed that when the officer confronts the boyfriend he is very combative and states that the act was consensual. Note that this individual is twenty-one years old. The officer must determine what type of crime scene he or she is investigating as well as what tactics the officer uses to place the subject in custody. Did the officer call for backup? Did the officer demonstrate proper tactics as well as officer safety protocols?

Call for a DWI

One officer stops behind a vehicle with a subject asleep at the wheel. While looking into the vehicle the officer observes a pistol and numerous beer bottles scattered around the front seat. The officer asks the driver if he is OK, at which time the driver is unable to respond and begins to slur his words. The officer assists the driver out of the vehicle at which time the driver falls to the ground and is nonresponsive. Note

THE BROKEN BADGE

how the officer questions the driver and attempts to perform a sobriety test. Also, note if the officer observed any physical injury to the driver. A federal marshal ID falls from the driver's shirt pocket. Did the officer contact communications and call for backup? Did the officer secure the firearm? Did the officer demonstrate officer safety skills while engaging the driver? Did the federal ID influence any of the officer's decisions?

68

CHAPTER 8

AUGUST 9, 2014: A NEW PARADIGM

RESPONSE TO THE FERGUSON UPRISING AND SUBSEQUENT POLICE RESPONSE

On August 9, 2014, in Ferguson, Missouri, Michael Brown, who was black, was shot by white Ferguson police officer Darren Wilson. Wilson's shooting of Mike Brown sparked tensions in the predominantly black city of Ferguson. Protests and civil unrest erupted. The events received a large amount of attention in the United States and around the world, attracting protesters from around the region. This incident sparked a national debate about the relationship between law enforcement and black Americans.

On August 4, 2014, I was promoted to my new position as Chief of Police for the city of Kinloch, Missouri. Kinloch borders Ferguson, and as such we were directly and indirectly involved in providing assistance as the rioting erupted. I had no idea how this rioting would redirect my efforts in police and community relations as well as police reform.

The rioting in Ferguson, Missouri, during the summer and fall of 2014 brought national and even international attention to the Mike Brown shooting. Subsequently, there was no indictment by the grand jury of officer Darren Wilson.

Because of the ensuing injuries, property damage, and arrests, the tactics employed by law enforcement certainly demanded scrutiny. The concepts of incident command, mobile field force, as well as mutual aid and other components that may have been underutilized all needed to be considered carefully.

From the community standpoint, the police response was overzealous, dangerous, and appeared more militaristic in nature. This alone seemed to ignite the protesters. As a result, the citizens created a nineteen-point rules of engagement for the police to review.

It must be mentioned that a riot/unusual occurrence is a fluid and unpredictable event. When analyzing the nature of these unusual occurrences, we think in terms of three levels of disorder:

1. Anarchy, urban terrorism, and violence
2. Active disobedience, unlawful assembly, riotous behavior
3. Passive disobedience, unlawful assembly, nonviolent behavior

Because of the police response in Ferguson and the heavily militarized presence citizens issued nineteen rules of engagement to the police. In this document the list calls for the preservation of all human life. Others in the community demanded that police avoid using riot gear and not react to protesters who hit police with bottles. Safe houses shall be considered sacred ground and only entered by police when called upon or if extremely necessary.

I would certainly hope no one would want an officer to receive injuries from an unusual occurrence when his or her injuries could have been mitigated by utilizing the proper equipment.

At the onset of a potential unusual occurrence and upon arrival of local law enforcement, incident command and emergency management should come online. Under the concept of incident command with the assistance of a multijurisdictional approach and mutual aid, all responding departments and officers will have a specific point of contact to receive assignments, equipment, and general orders.

The law enforcement incident command system streamlines the management of critical incidents by consolidating the response into modules. Vehicle collisions, pursuits, officer-involved shootings, natural disasters, and civil disturbances signify only a few of the incidents for which an agency can employ the law enforcement incident command system. Under those conditions involving multiple jurisdictions, LEICS (Law Enforcement Incident Command System) as a forecasting tool designates in advance the precise duties of all participants. Perhaps more important, it governs who will be in charge at the scene. Whether they need the response of one agency or many, critical incidents become more adaptable with LEICS. Anyone in the law enforcement community, from the chief of police or sheriff to the patrol officer, can implement LEICS into its complete configuration.

MOBILE FIELD FORCE

The mobile field force is a platoon-sized tactical force assembled from a percentage of department-wide, personnel assets in addition to mutual aid arrangements. The units respond in vehicle convoys with radios and field force kits. It allows rapid organization and a disciplined response to any unusual occurrence. It should be noted that all mobile field force officers have additional training in defensive tactics.

Specific missions that law enforcement may be involved in that may utilize mobile field force tactics would be:

1. Conventional crowd control situations within defined sectors
2. Patrol of hostile areas
3. Response to calls for service requiring multiple officers
4. Security for field personnel in hostile areas
5. Situations involving hostile crowds requiring chemical agents

6. High-profile patrol operations
7. Miscellaneous missions at the direction of the field commander

In addition, there should be reality-based training opportunities that include not only law enforcement, but should also include fire departments, city emergency management, EMS units, and local hospitals as this is a community-wide training opportunity. By training together, a more precise and effective response can be expected in the event of unusual occurrences in the future.

CHAPTER 9

REBUILDING TRUST: BRIDGES VS. WALLS

The training model, *trust in motion,* was developed to improve the relationship between law enforcement and the community. Often, fundamental trust issues are the root cause of many of the concerns that divide the community and the police. When members of the community see the police as an occupying force or an entity that does not have their well-being in mind, frustration, anxiety, and anger arise. The minute trust no longer exists, whether in police community relations, business, or a personal relationship, a void is created that if not repaired will make positive growth in that relationship doubtful at best.

If trust between the police and the community is eroded, the possibility of a successful and productive relationship is limited. Throughout history, especially American history, there has been a deep resentment between people of color and the police. Often this relationship is shattered and is soon followed by violence, anarchy, as well as a nonproductive and disheartening relationship. It is easier to build a relationship upon trust and fair play than upon fear and deceit.

When police officers operate in a vacuum and do not respect and value trust with the citizens in their community, their ability to get their work done effectively is limited. Imagine if the police and the community had a working relationship built on trust and fairness. How easy would it be for certain crimes to be solved as well as criminals arrested and held accountable? Many citizens will not cooperate with the police because they do not trust them and often fear them. This type of relationship often is a shattered relationship and does no one any good, wastes a lot of time, and is not effective. The goal of both the police and the community should be to build bridges and not walls.

Police officers who understand and value trust and the relationships they build with the community will relate to the following training concepts:

1. Articulate those situations that erode the trust between the police and the community.
2. Determine appropriate communication skills that would help diffuse conflict.
3. Define the concept of trust busters and how they influence behavior.
4. Discuss how to rebuild trust once trust a shattered.

Here are some definitions of terms used in those concepts:

Trustworthy

Taking responsibility for one's conduct and obligations as trustworthy public servants. Demonstrating a responsible nature worthy of or requiring responsibility, or being held accountable. Doing the right thing even if no one is watching.

Trust

To believe that someone or something is reliable, good, honest, effective, etc.

To believe that something is true or correct

To hope or expect that something is true or will happen

If employees don't trust each other or their leaders, all sorts of difficulties start to arise. Collaboration and communication stagnates, innovation ceases, worker engagement declines, productivity falls and, in general, the workplace becomes unsuitable to be in. However, today it appears everywhere we look there is a lack of trust.

Respect

A feeling of deep admiration for someone or something elicited by their abilities, qualities, or achievement.

In the wake of current events, there has been a call for new ways of constructing relationships with the police. Leaders want to deliver more ways for individuals to have a voice, work across divisions, and establish equitable policing that is answerable to the community. Where there is an erosion of trust between the police and community, it is difficult to create an opportunity to engage in productive dialogue.

Integrity

Firm devotion to a code of concepts and moral or artistic values. To do the right thing even if no one is watching.

Trust Busters

1. Doubts others
2. Promise breakers
3. Shows favoritism
4. Self-serving
5. Runs from issues

Event

1. Think of someone you do not trust
2. Think of someone you trust
3. Think of someone who trusts you
4. Think of someone who does not trust you

While reflecting on the above event concepts, ask yourself these questions: Is it possible for me to rebuild trust with individuals who no longer trust me? Am I able to establish trust with people who I lost trust with?

In the area of tactical communication, it is important to establish an opportunity to communicate with another individual who may be under stress, frustration, anxiety, or extreme anger.

Trust is a fundamental concept that, when established, creates a meaningful opportunity to work together with another individual.

As with trust, respect is also a fundamental concept. It is said that when referencing respect, I ask for no more and I will accept no less. As police officers, we often find ourselves juggling many theories, concepts, and procedures in order to establish a baseline of mutual respect and trust with the citizens we are sworn to protect.

Working with communities in town hall environments has been a very productive way to bridge the gap between law enforcement and the communities they serve. Having the community and law enforcement discussing issues and challenges, provides a forum for honest dialogue and a mechanism for resolution. The opportunity to involve both the community and law enforcement at the same time in a controlled environment under the watchful eye of a facilitator engages both groups toward a productive resolution of common challenges.

Quotations about Trust, Trustworthy, and Trustworthiness

Leadership requires five ingredients: brains, energy, determination, trusts, and ethics. The key challenges today are in terms of the last two, trust and ethics.
—FRED HILLMER

We need more people in our lives with whom we can be as open as possible. To have real conversation with people may seem like such a simple, obvious suggestion, but it involves courage and risk.
—THOMAS MOORE

*When people honor each other, there is trust established that
leads to synergy, interdependence, and deep respect. Both
parties make decisions and choices based on what is right,
what is best, what is valued most highly.*
—BLAINE LEE

*Trust men and they will be true to you, treat them greatly
and they will show themselves great.*
—RALPH WALDO EMERSON

*The glue that holds all relationships together, including the
relationship between the leader and the led, is trust,
and trust is based on integrity.*
—BRIAN TRACY

*The greatness of a man is not in how much wealth he acquires,
but in his integrity and his ability to affect
those around him positively.*
—BOB MARLEY

Trust but verify.
—RONALD REAGAN

Let me define a leader. He must have vision and passion and not be afraid of any problem. Instead he should know how to defeat it. Most importantly, he must work with integrity.
—A. P. J. ABDUL KALAM

Better to trust the man who is frequently in error than the one who is never in doubt.
—ERIC SEVAREID

The supreme quality for leadership is unquestionably integrity. Without it, no real success is possible, no matter whether it is on a section gang, football field, in an army, or in an office.
—DWIGHT D. EISENHOWER

The chief lesson I have learned in a long life is that the only way to make a man trustworthy is to trust him, and the surest way to make him untrustworthy is to distrust him and show your distrust.
—HENRY L. STIMSON

The leaders who work most effectively, it seems to me, never say I. And that's not because they have trained themselves not to say I; they don't think I. They think we, they think team. They understand their job to be to make the team function. They accept responsibility and don't sidestep it, but "we" gets the credit. This is what creates trust, what enables you to get the task done.
—PETER DRUCKER

Trust each other again and again. When the trust level gets high enough, people transcend apparent limits, discovering new and awesome abilities for which they were previously unaware.
—DAVID ARMISTEAD

We're never so vulnerable than when we trust someone, but paradoxically, if we cannot trust, neither can we find joy or love.
—WALTER ANDERSON

CHAPTER 10

CONCLUSION

It should be stated that the purpose of this book is an attempt to bridge the gap between communities and their police departments. This gap refers to the erosion of trust that exists between many police departments and the communities they serve. Often citizens question whether police officers are invested in their community or simply there as an oppressing force. My goal is to build bridges and not walls. Police work is inherently a dangerous profession and as such for those who are successful they must show a passion for this career.

The breakdown and erosion of trust between the community and the police department is something that must change to bring about a better relationship.

For me one of the primary areas of change must be *police culture*. Police culture in its very nature is very inclusive and generally only discussed among current or former police officers. It is my belief that if more police officers are held accountable for their actions, much of the negative behavior will cease. All too often officers who attempt to step in and stop another officer from engaging in some type of adverse behavior—be it excessive force or other types of issues—find themselves sanctioned by their department. These officers face the disdain of their colleagues as well as the possibility of transfer, demotion, or termination from their department. If officers feel that they will not be positively recognized for doing the right thing and stepping in to stop adverse actions by their colleagues, they most often will not commit themselves to be the agent of change that is needed.

The concept of one bad apple spoiling the bunch often is reflected in police departments around the country. Social media has shown time and time again officers claiming to have performed one action when the video that surfaces shows another. Cities across the country have witnessed this type of situation all too often. Police accountability is paramount and officers must be perceived as honest and trustworthy.

People of color, especially African Americans, feel that police departments are not receptive to their needs. Many African Americans believe their communities are under siege and their lives are not valued. Some believe that even when they comply with the officer's commands they still may face physical injury or death.

Certainly, there are legislative acts and legal sanctions that can change police behavior. I have seen three methods that generally change police behavior:

1. Officers are terminated or resign from the law enforcement profession.
2. Officers face legal sanctions and end up with lawsuits and financial judgements against them.
3. Training

It is my hope that if officers begin to self-check their colleagues—and if departments reinforce these good officers' behavior—real change may occur. How long before change takes place and communities believe their police departments support them is hard to say. But one thing is certain: if more officers step in and stop negative police behavior at the scene, at least that's a start. If officers follow the guidance and theories behind Lady Justice this, too, may help avert this situation. The International Association of Chiefs of Police oath as well as the various oaths the police departments have their officers swear to, if they were truly believed and followed, I'm sure we would see substantial change. It has been my experience that the clear majority of Police Officers report for duty and perform that duty with honor and professionalism. To those officers, I salute you.

CITIZEN REVIEW BOARDS

C itizen oversight is a form of citizen participation that reviews government activities. These activities may be identified as government misconduct. Members of the group are civilians and are external to the government.

A citizen review board is an entity external to the police department's internal affairs and consists of citizens from outside the department.

There is no single model of citizen oversight; however, most procedures have features that fall into one of four types of oversight systems:

1. Citizens investigate allegations of police misconduct and report findings to the chief or sheriff.
2. Police officers investigate allegations and develop findings. Citizens review and recommend that the chief or sheriff approve or reject the findings.

3. Complainants may appeal findings established by the police or sheriff departments to citizens who review them and then recommend their own findings to the chief or sheriff.

4. An auditor investigates the process by which the police or sheriff's department accepts and investigates complaints and reports on the thoroughness and fairness of the process to the department and the public.

The above information regarding citizen review boards and citizen oversight boards was taken from the U.S. Justice Department manual on *Citizens Review of Police*.

Citizen review boards, or civilian oversight, on the surface appear to be a great idea that could truly make a difference in how American policing functions. It has been my experience, though, that most citizen review boards do not contain the teeth necessary to be fully efficient. Most citizen review boards do not have subpoena power nor are they allowed access to all of the investigative material that police departments obtain. For citizen review boards to be effective there must be full transparency between the review board and the police department. Although there are some cities that have been able to utilize civilian review boards or civilian oversight boards the challenge is based on consistency and unbiased communications. At this point I have not seen that relationship fully developed, and as such what started out as a great idea does nothing more than give false hope to the citizens in the communities that need it most.

MAKE A NOTE

Police killed at least 102 unarmed black people in 2015, nearly two each week.

Nearly one in three black people killed by police in 2015 were reported as unarmed, though the actual number is likely higher due to underreporting.

In 2015, 37 percent of unarmed people killed by police were black despite black people being only 13 percent of the U.S. population.

Unarmed black people were killed at five times the rate of unarmed whites in 2015.

Only ten of the 102 cases in 2015 where an unarmed black person was killed by police resulted in an officer being charged with the crime, and only two of these deaths (Matthew Ajibade and Eric Harris) resulted in convictions of officers involved. Only one of two officers convicted for their involvement in Matthew Ajibade's death received jail time. He was sentenced to one year in jail and allowed to serve this time exclusively on weekends. Deputy Bates, who killed Eric Harris, was sentenced to four years in prison.

ABOUT THE AUTHOR

COL. KL WILLIAMS

As a police officer, it has always been my goal to work with communities and police officers to find solutions to very challenging police-community relations issues. It is very important to lead by example. In today's communities, we find a lack of trust and respect toward police officers on a day-to-day basis. I have worked diligently as a police trainer to work with officers to instill in them a sense of confidence and knowledge as it relates to the field of law enforcement. Although still a very dangerous occupation, police work offers challenges and opportunities like no other. I have traveled from coast to coast in America in pursuit of improving the relationship between law enforcement and the community. I realized early on in my career that in many communities there was an erosion of trust between the police and the communities they serve. Having facilitated numerous town hall meetings with the community, I believe that most citizens in the community seek answers to the challenges that exist between them and their local law enforcement. It is my hope that this book will serve as an opportunity for law enforcement officers and the citizens they serve to work diligently toward building bridges and not walls.

- Over thirty years' experience as a law enforcement officer
- Director of the Institute of Tactical Neutralization Techniques, Inc.
- Director of the American Police Citizens Academy www.apcitizensa.com
- Director of the Institute of Justice & Accountability www.instituteofja.com
- As a law enforcement officer, functioned as Chief of Police, Police Academy Trainer, Patrolman, Detective, and Emergency Management Consultant
- POST-certified law enforcement officer state of Missouri
- POST-certified trainer in Biased Policing / Racial Profiling / Alternatives to Deadly Force & Defensive Tactics
- State of Missouri Department of Public Safety Generalist Instructor
- Federal Bureau of Investigation Instructor Development Certification

- Instructor in Counterterrorism & Weapons of Mass Destruction SEMA
- Certified in Incident Command / FEMA
- Law Enforcement Field Training Officer Instructor Certification
- The Verbal Judo Instructor Certification
- DDI Instructor Certification
- DQE Decontamination Instructor
- Cooper Aerobic Institute Physical Fitness Coordinator
- Fit Force Peace Officer Fitness Coordinator
- Federal Bureau of Investigation Certified Defensive Tactics Instructor
- Advanced Taser Instructor Certification
- Phase Four O.C. Regional Certification
- Instructor in Use of Force / SLMPD
- Second-Degree Black Belt in Aikijitsu

Awards
POST Law Enforcement Instructor of the Year, Missouri
NAACP Arizona Man of the Year

Made in the USA
Monee, IL
07 November 2020